Dreaming Man, Face Down

poems by

Mark Conway

*To Mtn Don —
who turned Pine Knob
into the Himalayan.*

*Mark
12-14*

Dream Horse Press
California

Conway, Mark
    Dreaming Man, Face Down

        ISBN 978-1-935716-05-1
        1. Poetry

10 9 8 7 6 5 4 3 2 1

First Edition

    Cover design and artwork by Alan Reed

Contents

to samuel cullen liam

Dreaming Man, Face Down

Tarot Card of the Dreaming Man Face Down

Then it was gone, the beatitude
of your body,
        while the rest lay, specifically,
there: black, black,
blue, heavy
as a dead dog, the back
of your legs
looking plastic, looking extra, trailing
    behind the rest of you
like a mooch, like a goddamn moron and you
barely there,
     already camouflaging yourself inside
the light and dark, mouthing
       the prime numbers of eternity.

We gave you days to continue dying
               and you did
        after you were dead. We
needed time – poor relations
to arrive, to decide upon
the precise symbolism
of the flowers, to complete
the box, nail it into
position, to divest the body
of its slime, to call
your name three times;
to call you three times;
to call you by name three times.

And at first.
You wouldn't go.
    You own this body
    somehow
    thriving within the caucus
    of microscopic insects and dazzled

acids there to burn you down to ashes
you over there, you
in your over-there work-body
of the soul, your hooded
spirit released and humming
like its crazy in the light.

Where you are, slipping
through the monstrous
inner membrane of the world,
you see how it works.
I, like a mooch, like a goddamn moron, live.

We waited for you. Two or three days.
Then an old man came and prayed.

I.

Beneath Venice

City Out of Time

If you wake up
in a thickened hive of light,
and see the cypress,
eternal as the poor,
you know there's still a Rome
and the Tiber rides
between the sycamores
that split the Lungotevere
in the spit- and pissed-on shade,
Campo dei Fiore still exists,
the statue of its burned mystic broods,
the beam of his black intensity
similar to yours,
the way you stood, brooding,
before the cloaked figure
of yourself and found it
wanting.

+++++++++++++++++++

Remember your body?
        How it lay mornings in the tropics
of the Albergo Sole,
before it got up to part
    the beaded curtains and smoke
from a balcony, admiring
the echoing pavilions, all
the period décor of your last
and finite life.

+++++++++++++++++++

You'd see them,
from that body, dismantle
the daily set-up for the market,
and later it, the ecstatic it of you,
would soak up lemon-
juice and clams,
sucking dry wine
through its strong white teeth
and then lean back
into the last rags of light,
the air immaculate,
shining like bandages.

Zilch

That never happened. It did,
    but it didn't
  matter, it happened
in the time of blotto,
      of dust and nada, it was nothing
much, nothing
special –

    – it was the season before
the season of unknowing, the era
   of the Over-Answer:
that everything came to

naught.
       That was the time
        you were too
busy with your skull
        getting shrunken by the Swiss
     head-master, Herr Mindfüch, the nocturnal
       European pygmy, who nodded
sagely and said diddly
      in the still void
of rien. Then you started
    the old rumor Arabs
  invented zero – what's with you?
you never needed
  help to come up
with nothing before.

    Beneath the null weight
       of nadir, of zip, of nil,
the contours of your negative
   impression emerge – never &
     never
more a touch, an easy

turning of the face,
        everyone who dies adds
to the power
of zero.

            In your personal
        immensity, Employee
of the Year __, down below you see it: us,

like nothing in the jostling light,
        the routine dew
    burned out in the yellow zigzag
track of the day-
        drunk wasp.

Day of My Dead

so the cicadas drone louder
for the dead too
are busy

I believe in the communion
of the loving
and the bitterly forgiven

I saw you here
with these eyes
the eyes that swear

you're no longer
your body – it's true
your spirit didn't rise

out of its gray
casing but its smoke
rose into orange

trees and clock-towers,
cellophane
and trash autographed –

briefly – by a parish of bone
now divided
on itself – all

depends on the body, though
it's made to fail: still
the spirit remains,

stays as long as suffering
lasts, then seeps
away, but

while there it pays and pays
the surcharge
of pain, remains

like a dog, barking,
refusing to leave
its cold master:

and then you're surprised
to see the dead?
though they often arrive

in grocery lines, in six frames
of film, in part
of a face that turns

away and turns almost
into the face
you love,

not the one
you go down
toward in dreams,

another, bafflingly
alive, enjoying
its time

which rides behind
the present like a boat
its wave;

we close the eyes
of the dead
because they open again,

staring for us
up in the sky-filled instant,
eyes brimming

with rain, all that remains
from the time
of our fine passing

You Made Eternity

1.

folded Polaroid

You sat beneath
the eucalyptus, hovering behind
your eyelids while you smoked up
half a pack of Camels, you had it
all, rain

and the smoke sticking
fragrantly to your Camel-
colored breathing,
you were deep

in your contentment,
        one of
the supremes.

        Even then you were so neo-, no, no,
post-neo, nearly
fascist in formulating
the definition
of what made up
the sublime –

        you held to, what was it,
                a fairly *Egyptian*
    notion of the ultimate – death
as an opportunity
for fulfillment – a lead-in
to the extreme
extreme.

You taught me death.

Life was the exception.

I die because you die.

2.

You only feared a second-hand
dying where you'd drift
as gas through thrilling
          cosmic dust. You'd fan out
in a flattened universe
               of echoes annotated
into the book of going out into the day:
neo-death

you taught me neo-death.

We all will wind up singing in the green basilicas of grass.

We die because we were dead

always, before.

3.

We know death

but you worry
you'll be floating with
the ones who think
the proof of eternity
is silence...
maybe they should
just shut up

and enjoy the quiet just this
once,

can't they even
enjoy neo-
death?

  (but tell me, can you hear it,
        the spherical music,
  from your cell?)

you were no one to teach me life…

life compared to what?

Once dead stay dead.

4.

You made eternity
possible, beautiful as it careens
before us with
specific beards of wheat,
        proper-
nouns and rich options among
birds. Even heaven's filled
with more dead
lined up in corn rows
watching us & loving us,
elbowing to wave
to everyone on beatific
monitors, hello son, hello
my dear.

I die because you said it's easy

apparently, it's made for you.

I beg you:

re-consider;
           see, there's no life
but life

To You I Speak in Two Voices

Who am I to pray to
now that you're not
  hungry? I liked you hard-
      up, fairly
dirty, your need
for desperation
  your disease.
In the votive saucers,
sacrificial scraps rot
and now I hear nothing,
nothing
of your need.

+++++++++++++++++++++

How could I
hear you,
          locked
inside the cell-block
  of my iPod, wandering
  through your shrine?

At your altar, fatted
    candles spit, the icons lit
by the bad strobe
light of the cheap tallow, by its mule-, its pig-
        headed burning.
But in the inner dark,
          (shh)   all
  is well, all the good psalms
    smoking in
the greasy air.

    The gods are everywhere,
that's how we know them,
      by their exhaustion,
scraped so thin
you see through
each one beyond
to what is merely real.

++++++++++++++++++++

Are you praying, down
to us, are you
praying with your head
between your legs?
        I can't
hear you now, maybe you're speaking
through the dirt
        that used to be your
face, maybe
you can't be bothered
to remember
pain.

    Now I suppose you
have other hands,
other feet to walk amused
        above this canopy
we sit beneath – the sky, scraped
        immaculate, all
        that stands
between us and you.

Part-Time Lazarus

You were not born great
among the with-

holders, you learned to be great,
which gets you serious

traction, the law
of smalltown astro-

physics absolute: the depth
of attraction is equal

to the draw of the object
that can't be had,

a standoff that lasts
forever, or, right up

to the ignited, often
pharmaceutically-assisted

moment, then it's, whoa, lordy,
not so slow – so,

you could be

had, yet you had, as Ray said,
standards,

just set astonishingly
low, absolutely not

nothing, so they could be lowered
still. When she… and who

was she? The daughter
of a Gnostic,

you came to her,
a parolee from the Second

      Desire Wars, a non-
combatant with an aura

purchased at the local
spa, saintly kind of

down and damaged,
with the other-worldly sexy-feline

power of those risen
from the dead who say, please,

don't touch me

so she gets the oils and considers history
an intermezzo. See, she's

over there, chewing gum, getting lubed
with tears to wash you down,

look at her little head shine.

Ugly Bird Calls

In the far hills,
the peaks dark with dry trees
with figs stuck
to their stems like mystics
to their devotion, the villa
is built into
a hillside, way up
in Umbria, useless
for wine. From the top of the house
you can see past
the curve of the earth
and then up the coast, beneath Venice,
a shining city.
That one.
The city you can't come back from.

A blue jay or shrike
grates out some kind of cry, sounding
as though its throat's been cut,
a mating call
of distress and broken glass. Don't

laugh, I've seen it work, misery
as aphrodisiac.
You think no one goes
toward pain, but they do,
the slim girl slowly
toward her man shaking his hand
after punching out
the window, the crowds
pressing to get closer
to the crash, the hum
that comes off human blood.

Cars slow, medics in neon-yellow slickers
            slog through gas fires
        burning in the rain...
the air begins to swirl with fog and police-
            band static – the distorted,
hyper-beauty of what the archaic world
            looks like, just
        before it's lost.

After the After

Hear that redbird singing?
Soon it will rain,
   and the bird will remain a simple
       sub-atomic particle
of the physical divine,
even nothing
is God. This is the Lord

of my brother's late
conversion, the One who knows
      the sparrow's fall, but
  before that,
supported its art.

We're grateful
  for such attention
to detail, the carving
of each precise
bronze beak.
This one sits, still
as an icon in the black
devouring background, shining before
the eventual onslaught
of the orchard.
           God
of nothing, I like that.

High in the tree, the apple breaks
into annunciation: the white
flower is nothing.
It will appear
incarnate,
as juice, as sweet
and edible meat.

+++++++++++++++++++++

God of listening,
        of silence: If
the sparrow, then
the blood through its heart.
If the sparrow, the tree.

Pained by each leaf severed
from the stem,
each apple's fall,
He sits, witless in heaven,
frozen in the roar
of blasted brain cells, spills
of jism and spreading stains of oil,
bloodied bedclothes,
for the woman who prays
to die, who is not
helped.
                God
of nothing, he also weeps
for everything impossible
to exist.

+++++++++++++++++++++

And why not believe
in the God-besotted orchard –
why not be alive –
        at least to keep
the rusty hinges of the spirit swinging
open like a mouth?

We must eat and praise.

In the rush of generations
a wave of birds is crushed
beneath the soggy tonnage of the young
pushing on the orchard's edge,
pushing to be torn
into time. The sparrows praise
and loudly rise above
the mound of dead bodies,
walking up the heaped wings, singing,
clawing over the soggy breasts
and they praise, screaming with joy
stepping through the necklace of beaks,
loudly praising, while alive
they praise and praise
above all the birds
they sing, and while they praise
they live.

+++++++++++++++++++++

In our lovely hair and evening jackets
the adept
can smell the pollen of the Lord,
for though not everything
is God,
everything is
filled with God,
you can smell him,
you can taste him
you take him inside you
like smoke.

In the year of his conversion,
my brother met the saints
assigned to every speck
      of this pacific
cosmos, juntas of neutrons crammed
with god-stuff,
saints like sentinels bless each morsel.
Light beyond
light, soul of all souls and God nailed
to the core…
            Every corner holy,
      holy, this
    was the world.
This was the world he
died into.

II.

Lost in the Gardens of a State Resembling Perfect Being

No Apparent Marks

You gave that city
nothing. You left behind
    blurred snapshots shot
in the fanatic subjunctive –
  places you'd have lived (if
      you lived) as if
you cared: random
    landscapes – silver streets: the sea:
 German hookers: the sea:
        a ruin:
     jumbled in a shoebox, the way
 a tourist's thirst is satisfied
by knocking back
      another church, one
    more Etruscan site.

Across the piazza,
     pilgrims sing in a darkened crypt,
above them the gourmand
     desperately sucks
  his noodle.

You walked through them all
in your first rapture, chanting in a euphoric
  haze, the old life gone
     spinning through the crooked
transit of the sun. You, who died
  with your privacy
intact, had it happen
  here, so alone we barely know
the scene:
        the gun oiled
and cleaned, you took
  soul in hand,
    its hard rejoicing done.

When She Sang

she was anyone's —
                    the untamed glad young
            mezzo who
                        would have

what she wanted, and she was
        yours, once, but not
            long   because   for you
                                she lacked
                    the need to be
                            possessed or to possess
                                                        yes
                she was a fish
                        that swam in waters
            sweet or lightly
                    salted and she slept
with any eel
                    or trout or seal
        that made her cool
            or warm (in season)
                        and pleased her

        you learned her wants
                were always just a jump ahead
    of what everyone plus
                            you could guess at
                    or could attempt
to intercept
            in the angle of her choosing

and when she slept
                        with everyone
it made you feel
                    abused, you tried to make her
            love me

as it was the type of pain you found
amusing   until
she went along,
as you thought, but not
to please you. she turned
eyes cool, fairly green,
calm as Kant
critiquing reason
and I looked down to see
we'd already begun
to rise.

I kissed her or her
me just inside
the first ring of the inner
city while the night, politely,
held its breath in a moment
of unexpected
tact. And now or then

she lives in Ghent
or on the Ganges and you live always
inside time
where everything remains
but nothing
can be recognized.

Still-Life of Dreaming Man with Autopsy

After the trepanning,
the skullwork, following
your removal from

this life, you ask why I keep
looking at
the dead, in the gaps

that were your eyes, why
I make
a fetish of your hair, the stuff

that grew while
you are gone. Who are you
to tell me

anything, dead
man? I say to
you, looking at the blank

form in the slightly over-
weight man's
foreign office.

You know you aren't
going anywhere,
I tell you

softly – You aren't
going anywhere –
I shout in our minds,

– so don't think
you can tell me
to move

on.

That Was When You Lived

That was when you lived
    above, beneath the frenzy
of the belfry and its nazi-birds strutting
    and sprechen pigeon in the wind
outside the window. That was
    exactly

    where again? ah, yes, up
        there in the alcove
of the universal, where you walked
    amuck
    in the confines
of your gorgeous little mind. Son,

you were generally
    aflame in
the folded honey-comb
and deep-fried brain
    of that comedic master: Self-as-
Major-Structure,
but

come on everyone

knew you were hot and vivid
in the cerebral
cortex. Yet you
    had to keep on loading in
    free adrenaline: fear and Derrida,
abject babes, long
    espresso-trains – it was some
fun – not to mention
the reliables – white
crosses, white rum, dum dums hmm more fun

anything to stay there, swinging
from the rafters

31

of your souped-up skull,
to see what's, more
or less, exactly out there, hard
to pull off
armed with just a disappearing line
of flake and a 3 lb. brain.
Not that

you didn't like
your body: oh, no,
you threw it milk
bones, treated it to dishfuls now
and then again
to a coalition of lukewarm hot-
entots and sent fat fingers
of scotch down to the Nixon Library,
Dick's Honkytonk, drinks
all around, Mr. President, all around
the cellar of the inner sun.

What came to an, ah, un-
doing was, in fact, the lack
of the Actual, the matter
of the big

picture – you
were visited by the real
like St. Francis
was by birds. That is:
miraculously. That is, not.
every. day…. Yet

you were luminous
in your confinement… I saw you
gently holding yourself

away, the way a lover
                makes her body
    known, held
above, like breath, in the first intake
        of wanting, held high,
    like clothes
while crossing the river.

            What did St Francis say
in the middle of the birds' conversation?
            All we know
is that he raised his arms.
        They came to him,
and while they talked,
                he tried to stay
not quite human.

Ideogram of the Dreaming Man Lying Down (With Book)

You read whole days
   in no-
time, in mid-
air, days made of Vico, the Sufis
and Russian

despair, you read the blue rain of Burgundy,
hyper-aware, no relief
from the *one-that-reads*
or the sense

you would find enough
pages to replace what's there
and not there, over where
the technicians
of desire
placed it. You could have been
anyone, but you pored
through the Borgias
like a scholar of orgies,

through the history of space,
checking off Byzantium,
Li Po and the later
Spinoza, in flames yet always
sequential, you burned
from Adorno through
Zola.

You read with
your clothes off
in a deep vegan-
delirium with the idea
     of the one annulled

by the volume of the many
    as you edged
away from the only one
you knew, who endures now
    in pictures, mouth
closed as a book.

Maybe One of the Saints

Envy him
who's dead was
what the Romans

said. Pretty cold,
and manly – almost like
they didn't know

they were plagiarizing
the Greeks, again –
but still. Burly,

and slightly
deranged, the way the Romans
like their

virtues.
And believe me,
I never

envied my brother,
even now
he's dead though

this raccoon-like
scrabbling through
his clothes, washing

and re-washing
the wan
body, then numbering

the relics
is a bit
much, I know.

++++++++++++++++++++

But I only want
to know him,
the parts

cut away
in me that grew
in him, maybe

more manly, almost
Roman. About the picture
that emerges

of our father, poor
guy? A suburban
jefe but

Jim I think
loved him, well, at least
through puberty

and I suppose I did, that
much, too. Jim
never put our

father down,
even as he shrinks
in what is now

euphemistically called
real time, though
it would be nice

to think his vices
contract
at the same rate,

in that sense of
compensation
Nature

is rumored to have,
I see
father's sins dry

as sugar, dried
into veins
of fossilized wishes

some fantasy
of doing right
by us. Well.

I still hope
for mercy and one day
he may be forgiven,

maybe by one
of the statues he loved
so much,

some Irish saint, the patron
of rage, omelets,
gimlets and

maybe insurance.

Apprentice in Black

You were always the most
faux devout

convert, eager for any whiff
of arcana.

I haven't seen you
in years,

I jumped

when I picked out your head,
almost shaved,

dented in the right upper quadrant
with the signature

scar. The beam
of your smile's the same

as you turn to me, put down
your Galoises,

grinning, the poised, smoking
acolyte.

++++++++++++++++++++

We embrace
and I'm back, fallen, again

for your style. But then
I'm accustomed

to your virtuosic conversions,
this time knocked

down in your Florentine
flat
              by the visitation

of a silent, obscure
saint. It's the standardized

vision that makes me
suspicious –

… this time, is it real?

+++++++++++++++++++++

We walk beneath the Roman
pines and I guess

it's your passable
Greek that intrigues

the Black Monks hungry
for postulants. You get a cell

on the Aventine,

three meals and a ring-side

seat on the divine.
You've taken to waking

at four in the morning to kneel
at the window,

singing your office while the Tiber
falls. You say

you feel cleansed, not yourself,

but another, an envelope of ether

poised over the river. I try to believe it

as you, ether and brother,
pick a piece

of tobacco from your lip.

+++++++++++++++++++++

We've walked through the green
Aventine streets to the clean sanctuary

where I leave you.

You walk the field toward the abbey,
your new cassock trailing

in the high weeds.
                    In the dark,

you've no legs,
the grass carries you along.

In Your Ancient City

I tried to know the city
where you lived alone,
        where you let us glimpse you
through antique postcards you sent
with rants against
        your superstitious landlord.
    I've finally
    found the romantic address
(*Vialle Stefano Giudice*)
    and then a box of shirts
untouched in the closet.

        Cedar and cat-piss, that's
the last of this world
you took with you, the smell of that room
        with side-
views of umbrella pines
washed in the clear grappa
light of January, all the exotica
we lost you in.

        Of the three ways you left us:
through the intellect;
through the shoulders of a thin green bottle;
through silence on the long retreat;
I'm sure the coldest
was the first.

        So that's your life,
silence. It's the way
I hear you, now
you can't say a word.

But is that really
it? …

the way you occupied
a haircut, your once-
famous silhouette blown
to bits?

You were always
        going nowhere
in particular, taking up the guitar,
then muscles
and a leather vest,
    a few moods
you picked up and then put down.
I get happy
and then lose the way,
        you said, *I think that's as close*
as I'm going to get.

If I could ever see you again,
your life come back in a bird,
your face somehow appearing in a cloud,
I could show you:
        Look, this

is what you left behind –
    that exact cloud,
that very fucking bird.

III.

The Roman Way of Death

Having Gone to the Ends of the Earth

The Romans had a way
to talk to the dead: bring them
a bowl of blood.
But the blood
must be warm, which means,
it must be yours.

Hard to tell if the Romans
found this amusing,
but holding the long-desired face
between hands
that suddenly feel
nothing is difficult for some to accept – others

find the whole scene over-
done. Mind if I ask
what you'd do,
given the chance?

For the luxury-loving Romans,
of course their hell
is cold, maybe
I could go down there,
that may be my
type of suffering. It's true

I've always wanted
to know my brother, the one
just ahead of me,
the one with a talent
for disappearing
before he could be
interviewed; his genius
was being somewhere
else.

Now that he's through
the three doors,
the people of Rome
claim him as theirs:
They washed out the house;
they sang over the remains;
they processed to the field.

Now the ritual's done,
his body's no longer confused
with his soul – even
a Roman theologian would agree:
my brother's dead, to us,
and to Rome.
     He was helped
through the doors.

Suburban Eden

In front of us the sea, behind,
    the hard South, nailed
            to the thin heel of Italy. Down
        the harbor lights drifts Brindisi,
    lost city of the dead, the end
of the Way.

                And who
are the dead? The usuals:
                irregulars
    and strangers, Roman soldiers in minor
Thracian wars, tourists
        ferrying to Greece or
back.
        That's what they get
    here, the nobodies, and Virgil,
        dying, dead, in his tracks.
                The Appian Way ends
 in steps down to the harbor,
    which means it's the way
        East and the way
back, if you're dead
you can't miss it.

+++++++++++++++++++

Cash machines, hashish
and geo-trash
tourists, seekers and fakers here
for the night, cheap
passage to Greece and what's
next. Eyeballed by exiles
who know the best
bars for lounging and picking off
the weak: those wounded in loneliness,
those who sing
and groove.

+++++++++++++++++++++

This isn't the place
for exile. Cheap-ass expats
distill vineyards
into cheap flats, where they live
together, in stylized
regret.   For them, it was lovely, lovely, though
    the bottom
of the sack. Exile's a mild form
of forgetting.

      They've opened views to radiant
     groves of artichokes,
   where farmers strip
       enormous
green fronds until they reach
   lush central fruit.
     Waste is a luxury
learned from the Greeks.

Behind us, the white space
   of the sunset,
the sky erasing the West
while we look to Greece.
    Each night the stars re-enact
  scenes from the *Iliad* early
in the oriental sky.
      Why bother
with the sunset? The exiles clap and shout
  for Agamemnon, they whistle
for the spears.
      We waste
the other stars like time.

The Persistence of Six O'Clock

It's the hour you went over
and disappeared into gin;
the cocktail hour, well of course.

If you'd return to take up our city,
we could lie into the length
of a dry evening, I could listen

to your long unfinished myth.
We'd sit back and hear
the venereal laughter of teenagers

smoking in the pines. They smolder
on the verge of gray, moving
to the slipstream of the spring narcotic,

coughing as the night divides
between the trees. It's like this
for you, I know, six o'clock

glowing with stolen cigarettes
then out, the dusk gone bourbon.
We'd see a processional of lights

move off into the woods, the children
gravely demonstrating their bare chests
while beyond them other cities burn.

There is much we haven't seen.
The still, imperfect air is marred
by streetlights, a smudged bird.

A girl drops to her knees,
looking for a light, or hurt.
Or maybe she's in love.

Santa Maria Sopra Minerva

Once again you lived above
your ways and means, atop

two fascist embassies
with a perfect view

of jewelry near the Spanish Stairs.
Your flop was high

above the Bank of Rome,
the flat deserted by the Peruvian

princess with her deft
Andean lips and a tongue

that licked whipped cream
off daily with the delicate zeal

of the recovering. The rooms
were vast

and marbled like the past
you wish you had,

one that in the diorama
of the fourth-grade brain

looked entirely Roman. Declan said
you ate uncooked

potatoes when they turned
the gas off in the sadness

of the princess's hasty
deportation

and you squatted there,
shoulders hunched, gently

chewing. The balcony gave out
to the seven precise palms

that spear the heart of Rome
with a view of pilgrimage

hotels filled with Northerners
devoutly worshiping

room service. But you chose
the rear and birds

above the dome of Santa Maria
Over Minerva,

perfect for you, always
a type of ancient

in your reverence for the cold
and dead, especially

when it removes you
from the moment.

You loved the church-as-Circus-
Maximus

where each new deity impales
the one before it.

When Christ's mother
murdered gentle

Minerva, she wrote
her own name

above the porch and on the adjacent
obelisk.

That's what inspired you, the pagan
promise of salvation:

you will endure;
you will be cobbled over.

We Were Expendable

We can no longer walk to the Asia or France
of our Glorious City,
to its bakeries and flower stalls
with you, because you've already left us
the corpus, the past opus
of your flesh, now
no matter where you deign
to exist, how high the moon and grand
the heaven you dwell in,
you can't see
the way I can

how beautiful was the city of the living
this afternoon,
in a November of deep degree, one
of the collected days.

Now we have to love you
without having you,
without even wanting you and
and on top of that
you're dead.

Scholar of the Sorrows

I'm afraid of nothing but the world my son
will take over, don't think I'm not caught
like all the rest. I just don't want him here

watching the thin men memorize the sorrows.
Unforgivers, they sit in dark cafes,
their endless clubs and halls, stirring

beers, mumbling, calling out small dreams
of violence: how they ought to, should have,
tossed out the wife, knocked the shit out

of the neighbor. They're doomed to remember
and rage, rage and reminisce. They sleep
like horses, standing, and keep their teeth

in kerosene to be reminded of revenge. And
I'm one of them, a gifted scholar of the sorrows.
I remember, I'll always remember you.

But why worry, my son can't see the gray men
invisible as pigeons. He's taking in the Campo
like there's no tomorrow. He's heard the latest

revolutionary rumors: that his parent's imperial
order will soon be overturned. He can feel his youth
come in and is free in the complete indifference

of Roman time, both of us off the map and wandering.
We eat in the old shops, play and beat on
the same crooked pinball machine, I watch him

watch the lovely woman walk her sweatered pug.
She's Roman, young, severely chic, a slender
polytheist out adoring the dusk and blue swifts

writing hieroglyphs in the wind above the Tiber.
Who could worship a god who doesn't love
the other gods? My son walks these paths

I walked with you, I adore the forms
the world puts on: eyes and mouths set above
a pantheon of necks and tanned chests,

a blur of endless changing faces, smoking,
standing in front of more faces, arguing
and eating. I adore the obstinacy of objects

that put on Renaissance facades and the sweaters
of dogs, then lose their features in the endless
rub and interrogation of the Tiber.

I look up, see my son leaning against
a wall of Etruscan rust and ivy. Near the corner,
children wash a Fiat at the local fountain.

A parrot sits on the smallest girl's shoulder,
swearing slowly, *cazzo, stronzo, cazzo,* as the car
begins to shine inside a shield of ancient water.

Boilermakers on the Prairie

In the cornfield, mid-July,

thunderheads threatening
from off the Dakotas,
we live

with our boots on

walking miles of corn out
on the plains endless
as sweat —

we're headed to the windbreaks, rows

of swaying cottonwoods, the only place
they keep shade
around here. We drink

in the dark till it's cool in the night,

then drive with the lights off, eight of us
packed in the Ford,
steering by the glare

of winter wheat and the light put out

by stars and cheap beer,
we tear through sweet-
clover flats dark in the dream-life of plains

as we thrill to our ghost-selves pounding

straight toward us, driving by the face
of the moon,
those famous riders, our doubles, us,

ourselves from the West

locked in the same acres of summer and boredom
with being young,
electroshocked by the same R&B

and we're bobbing our heads

in opposable fates, we've known
they've been coming,
lights off, identical drunks

headed this way and from high above

you can hear the melodious
cars drawing nearer
and the faces get whiter

as we hammer the drum of the vinyl seats,

nodding to the music, to each other,
eyes wide, shining,
only the red

of our hearts beats out

Not Night

Cottonwoods bring down
the sun, suck the sky bone-blue,
    then load the light
       inside sapwood
      and stones. Now the way
is lit for mink, barred owls, those
     who eat the weak by dark.
          The nude horizon gleams
like gutted fish.

     Way up there dark
plum clouds push the sopped
air down, the prairie
on edge while sheet lightning writhes,
      breaking slightly
free of the sky …

    Watch the dogs' noses up,
      the wind getting raw
and lean. Out there the river, the one
    that never ends,
scrolls to the west, quartering off
   to where the Dakotas
reside. Look: nothing. Then,
nothing. Hey, have
a seat if you want to see
      this long night-
fall, goddamn it, I said,
don't blink or you'll miss it, over
   here, I said,
it's all but dark.

Visiting the Office of What's Left

I was here... once
before, I remember the little
man, broken, in
        the station,
    stingy rain and crests of oil-
filled brown waves
    breaking. Yes, the beach,
trashed with Slavic syringes
and Turkish condoms, so much
  the police ran out
and sang: No one swim.

        I could claim your body since
I was your brother
    as I suppose
I'm still next of kin (though
I imagine you now
have other types
of kin). We were told

we could burn the body
for ease of shipping, or
we could grease
the minor palms of
invisible officials,
        we had options,
we had many ways
to make grief
more insane and bitter
in the mouth.

Has Been

If you're dead
and you

are,
go back to the forest
where they make
the green
trees
that burned you, go back
to the smoke;

you can
go

inside.
What's your problem,
that it goes
away?
Heaven is nothing,
a small place,
a small price
to pay for being,

and you my friend
have been.
It's said

some even
cling, I mean
until cleavers
lop their red
talons at the wrist,
        I meant

in vain
they gripped
to stay,
here.

IV.

ascension into north dakota

Tattooing the Dreaming Man (Post Mortem)

These are all the words that can be written on the body.
On the face and chest,
the back already gone to red clay, rot,
ruined for writing.
These are all the words that fit on the evident body,
on the slate, legible surface,
chassis and chasuble, the neck and scapular heights,
pistons, root ends, cliffs.
This is the lot visible on the zinc counter, lying,
as it were, in state.
And these are all the words that fit on the misshapen self,
all that can be written
by needle-gun and ink; this much, then you're plainly
out of room.
This, then, was the body.

+++++++++++++++++++++

These are the words the body writes.
Face. Wound. Hair. Grin. Spit. Blood. Lips. Dream.
The face is written by wind tattoos, the slow
      claw that scars
the cheeks of the middle-
aged, the almost-aged, the old. The skin writes, "Man
is the animal whose face
withers" and though these clichés
don't sell, still
it writes. Its vellum pages
are marked with broken blood,
small crow's-
feet: inscriptions proof
that we'll sit still, dumb
with living, unable to move
the grief-tongue – even
in front of the sorrowful mother.
      But you, quite rare, are under-
done: no worry-lines, though you shine
with a light liquor-tan. Strange,
since you tended toward the ornate, the sublimely
over-written:
This, then, was your face.

++++++++++++++++++++

The merchant neck runs the food canal down
to the twisted gut – the neck
         is the way we know regret:
a means to look around, but not, entirely,
back. A difficult estate,
proud and small,
room enough for elegy, nothing
more:
This, then, was the neck.

+++++++++++++++++++++

I write on the chest with Heimlich shots to wake
the body up, the waked corpse.
The chest is written in wine and yellow,
creeping black, smeared blue bruises
and fucking rouge on sewn-shut lips.
Old friend, the chest, the machine we beat with fists
to beg forgiveness of,
its vast armoire
stuffed with post-it-notes and motor oil,
it stores the beaten heart, and
this one's done – crushed, white
as lard in lieu of
confiscated blood.
This, then, was the chest.

+++++++++++++++++++++

The waist is where the body begins to break
in two, narrowed, belted like
the cheesecloth sock of whey
we used to put out to clobber, I mean,
get hard. If it could bend, then it
could bow, say thank you sir
for all you've done:
This, then, was the waist.

++++++++++++++++++++++

And this is the gut that lacked the rum
that took the food
and spun dung from straw,
it mucked the barn for nothing at all
and growled and barked
and turned the crank, made itself
both grist and mill,
it didn't dwell on what it lacked,
took what it got and ate it all,
a hired hand, a trusted man,
this then was the gut.

++++++++++++++++++++++

I write the legs that write the end, feet
turned, awkward – pigeoned – in,
legs designed to rescue you
weigh you down, made of mud.
They lead the way at the cart's front,
gently bounce as you're wheeled back
to the final room where the oven stands,
chaste air-brushed chrome,
where all who've died will rise again
in blue, industrial flame.

Before the Perpetual, the Bottomless Light

Having come through this life,
exhausted, done,
you meet, walking toward you
        through the high ryegrass,
                the fabled body. It's the one
you have to put on
        again, forever. For the joyous banquet,
            or the reckoning, maybe
both. You're shocked

at seeing your old friend,
how little you feel for Dave
            or Mary Lou, whoever the hell you were.
You barely recognized yourself ...
but how could you have,

you really let yourself go.
        Yet you smile, got to
hand it to Dave for making it
this far, you shake your head
        and laugh at all
you two went through.

Here he comes, but...
        what's there to say? Um, er,
    hullo—? Plus: little Dave
        shows signs of the rye-field.
                Look

at all those holes. Help me

understand the body, what it's an instrument
of. I woke up
near the river, I drank
    the iron-stained water.
Now it's time to go.

+++++++++++++++++++++

So why stay and listen
        to Dave yammer on about the blah-blah everlasting,
you know the body's
always quick
to lie, given
to such outrageous claims:

before the evening fire it says
we'll never die maybe
others but not us boss not
us this moment
will never end

while inside the drowning heart
suffocates in blood – it's
the only part we trust

because it talks to us,
crying, confessing
its despair –

it pounds its heavy fist
against itself,
beating on its iron-
chambered walls:

done un-
done done
undone done
undone....

[And I rose early and walked through the fields that were]

And I rose early and walked through the fields that were my century, stunted woodlots and corn-fields, the claptrap of dreams, and so on, id-blood, etc., walked again through the fabric of the way I see, the optics of the usual, without – and this hardly needs to be said – seeing: the pastures' inner structure pent-up, made manifest (mostly green), supported by granite and the unusable sky, poor clay;

And I went out with urgency for I had lain in bed a long time with my wounded dreams, the fall of the house of glass and such, even while great rafts of teal and wood-ducks descended often, sweeping through the small sky of these woods (oak and birch) and as I walked I was vain enough to be in my heart fulfilled weirdly, filled as it was with grief;

And I went to the river unmoving, the river like a snake with glittering current twisting sluggishly through the heat of August, lulling even the afternoon sleepers, their humid dreams, to slow, and I cast a plug into the back pool wholly still, nothing moved in the windless day until the bass, green-backed, wine-red in the mouth, rose and brought the river back in to life;

And I spent most days badly, not even walking, not even looking at the gulls and geese that besieged my brown fields, a hundred and twenty acres of once-rich bottomland, the fields broken, prone and pleading to their lordship, me, for Christ's sake, me to harvest them, with all the terrifying machinery I can't run; most days so dead and useless, I tried to squeeze a bit out of them, but without much effort, like those boys that hang themselves part-way to get an extra kick from coming, the sick thrill of the noose;

And underneath you sleep, underneath the weight of implied snow, retiring in your roman purple, in lurid robes that demonstrate with crude assurance where and when the life went, out, flesh broken-down sweet to sugar ants, the legions rapt, attentive the way no woman ever loved you, an army absorbed in your contextual honey, burrowing up past wicker sinew, beyond tendons into sacs of fat, yellow lard, you know these are your fields I walked through, the ones carved by your hand, the lands you knew so well:

76

Halo, Sun-dog, What Have You

                    o most adept
& rococo empire, it's time
                        to leave
& leave you to
your sea-views & minor caesars
the ones that pleased me
and those that rendered me

down to suet. I'm not saying
it wasn't pleasant,
coming in from out
            the desert, almost
saved by lines

of lyre-inflected
music, that counts
for something, sure.
                The delegation
doesn't mean to
        sound ungrateful,
but some have more
            than a tin can full
                    of piss for memory.
We recall…
                the pillage,
    & the villagers rampant,
                    fleeing, Jesus,
it was something.
            All in all it made me

need-dazed, on my knees to its
            Byzantine, electric, most
majestic 4/4 time, all that:
    & more
worlds to come.

It was head-whirling, really,
ravished & get this:
I was wholly
cored in preparation for
            the mystic

abyss — why not,
it sounded fairly sexy,
            though still a little
queerball: was it similar
        to the inner blindness lauded
often by hermits, the shit I rescinded
            in the time I wasted on the prairie — what?
am I saying?
wasted: I killed it,
watching cable. That's what
I went in for, in
            installments: debauching
on the pay plan, barely
        paying attention.

& now all over. It comes
down to: buttes & sage,
        the great plains I lived
on, or, definitely, with… I'd had
        a chance to be enlightened,
in the western
        fashion (mini-bolts
            of lightning, head
                    fires, naked
        dashes through
the noonday, etc),

but missed it: all I see
from my lookout

on the prairie is a summer
highway: hot
tar & s lines of ever-retreating...I'd say,
liquid: my lovely
fake oases.
& there with it
is my small heat flaring in the distance:
whoa,
look at it go, sun-
down.

++++++++++++++++++++

deposition

the men, built well and
strangely bent, twist, and – bending – flex
though they only comfort the grieving
mother. she who was His mother. is.
now you see the young, brute shoulders
polished like maple turned on the renaissance
lathe of light.
vanishing point; depth of field; false flesh.
look at them go
nuts: scarlet tunics & peagreen cloaks & and give them
why not, a beret, make it
any color in the riot of the italian twin inventions:
humanism and high fashion, but you
already know the plot: He's
dead, condemned days ago.
playing out the hand:
His passion was to
tolerate & outlast reality
then to rise
3 days from now, stiff, gored,
divided hardly any-
more, additionally
divine.

when I
died and left I saw you
all, dwindling
at my bed. brown and gray and… so much
less vivid than I thought.
still, I wanted
eyes.
oh. the televangelism of your exaggerated loving…
the realpolitik of grief – my time
hardly complete and you
bury me.

lull

turning back – relenting –
is often better
than the leaving…though,
     I've used both
to get my way.

    departing, going, getting
on the highway,
       an exhalation of regret
           like just-cut, dead
hydrangea floating
in thick water... it gives off
a scent of forged nostalgia –
that this moment
lasts, that beauty's severed head
of petals somehow persists,
and will give pleasure.

and so one turns back…
and turns again,
to go.

+++++++++++++++++++++

now the going,
the leaving unimpeded,
shaking the dust off the serape
     is just joy,
going, gone, owing no one nothing, and
if I did, try to

make me pay.

no, this time
let the lips stop,
let them close my eyes with coins, cover
my cheeks with reverential, scared-
shitless kisses,
I'm the vapor leaving,
though I appreciate the gesture,
I really do.

        bee-stung stunned lips, the crimson
I kissed her with, slits
   in velvet that opened
  in a tongue of put-out flame,
raw thickened flesh that licked
  the deepest draughts
of honey and air and her careless
throat...
           and I'll miss:
   all of it, the kind
of love practiced here, where
you balance at the breakfast nook
with cantaloupe and coffee spoons,
     looking at the intent,
known faces casually telling out
  the news – plans
for swimming later on, a just division
of the cars, how my dying made you feel
first this, then that.

ascension into north dakota

past empty towers, through
burnt bonfires,

past cold soot settling
on chicken coops,

slats of sunlight lengthen
to the east, creeping up

the hard wheat, durham,
and the just-hoed soybeans – we

go down. to the north,
geese get fat

on field corn, ready to
abandon manitoba.

leaving let's you love
what's left

behind: mud-
rutted backroads,

broken-down
back-hoes, the creaking

derrick lifting, see
the eaves of yew trees drinking

in the sun,
and I glide, receding, drifting

inside the sky inside the soil
of north dakota,

the land itself nomadic –
rich silt built

by the great red river each spring,
delivered and dumped.

I see the few eyes lifted
in fargo to the sunset, my people

who love last things,
look at their eyes, glinting,

a glass reflecting the used-up evening,
and it's back, this day

flaring briefly in their eyes:
that's the way, I see,

I'm going.

++++++++++++++++++++

down through muck,
through troughs of sandstone,
past night-crawlers, nuptial
and velvet in their coiled nests,
        past soaked dust,
    we move through sand
and shining mica, majestic,
cut deeper into the canadian shield,
    its gong of granite,
iron and rust

you will come through

this is our body

music of the daughter, evening,
the harp of the heart bursts in the density
of dirt and still
you keep on falling
crawling down toward time

+++++++++++++++++++++

sweet smell of sweat, burned tea, burned salt

stars of crystal in my hair

li po in his slippers whispers
        to us, the drifting, his love
of dying, that we shouldn't fear
the book of evening
encased in frost,
        blank cover older than the sky, dark
and gleaming
in eternal dirt

spare moon torn like skin

body wasting like the moon

down through schist, no more
than dust, pulling down
        our sun, magnificent,
    the going down,

entering the slow
               factory of stone

matter-less and light, I move
               through vaulted limestone
     where gothic domes rise, bone-white,
to undergird horse-rich flatlands,
               where burned oat fields
lap at the limits of bismark;
          heaven open at our floor.

+++++++++++++++++++++

I thought I'd need
your face, or would make it,
make myself
a copy, serene, serener,
make a graven icon and hide it
in the infinite

folds of our newly eaten body, paradise
must have idols:
          there should –
if there's mercy –
be room for what we've known

          still, we long
for the body we have,
          giddy, erratic,
stoned, we rise
     in pitch, smashed like waves
to foam, still longing,
          we sing for the god
we are, in our head
          immediate light

Acknowledgments

Grateful acknowledgment is made to the editors of the following journals, anthologies and websites, where versions of these poems first appeared:

Agni: "Not Night."
American Poetry Review: "Day of My Dead," "You Made Eternity," "After the After," "When She Sang," "Maybe One of the Saints" and "Suburban Eden."
Alaska Quarterly Review: "Zilch" and "Part-Time Lazarus."
Center: A Journal of the Literary Arts: "Ideogram of the Dreaming Man Lying Down (With Book)."
Drunken Boat: "Apprentice in Black."
Harvard Review: "Scholar of the Sorrows."
Luna: "Boilermakers on the Prairie" and "Has Been."
Memorious: "Visiting the Office of What's Left" and "lull."
Slate: "Tarot Card of the Dreaming Man, Face Down."
Swerve: "In Your Ancient City."
Third Coast: "Still-Life of Dreaming Man with Autopsy" and "That Was When You Lived."
Tifferet (on-line): "City Out of Time."
Valparaiso Poetry Review: "Having Gone to the Ends of the Earth."
The Walrus: " [And I rose early and walked through the fields that were]."

"Halo, Sun-dog, What Have You" won the dA Center for the Arts 2008 Poetry Contest; [And I rose early and walked through the fields that were] won the 2008 SLS Kenya Contest judged by Anne Lauterbach. "Scholar of the Sorrows" was republished on *Poetry Daily* and "Having Gone to the Ends of the Earth" will appear in the anthology *Poetry from Paradise Valley*, to be published by Pecan Grove Press.

Thanks also to the MacDowell Colony, the Corporation of Yaddo, and The Villa Slackjaw for space; to the McKnight Foundation, the Jerome Foundation and the Minnesota State Arts Board for time; to the College of Saint Benedict for research assistance; to the many friends who helped get these poems on the page; to Alan, for his inspired designs; and again, as always, to Therese. Also, in memory of Chris and Peter.

About the Author

Mark Conway's book *Dreaming Man, Face Down*, was awarded the 2009 American Poetry Journal Book Prize. His previous book of poetry, *Any Holy City*, won the Gerald Cable Book Award and was short-listed for the PEN/Joyce Osterweil Award for Poetry. His work has appeared in *The Paris Review, American Poetry Review, Slate, Ploughshares, Bomb, The Grolier Poetry Prize Annual, The Boston Review* and elsewhere. He lives in Avon, Minnesota and is the Executive Director of the Literary Arts Institute at the College of Saint Benedict.

CPSIA information can be obtained at www.ICGtesting.com
Printed in the USA
BVOW020701240512

290968BV00001B/70/P